THE ASTONISHED HOURS

Books by Peter Cooley

The Company of Strangers (1975)
The Room Where Summer Ends (1979)
Nightseasons (1983)
The Van Gogh Notebook (1987)
The Astonished Hours (1992)

THE
ASTONISHED
HOURS

Peter Cooley

Carnegie Mellon University Press
Pittsburgh 1992

ACKNOWLEDGMENTS

Acknowledgment is gratefully made to the editors of the following magazines in which these poems or versions of these poems first appeared:

AMARYLLIS, "Satisfactions"
THE ANTIOCH REVIEW, "Little Ode"
THE ATLANTIC MONTHLY, "Mother and Child"
CALIFORNIA QUARTERLY, "In Advent," "Sext" (as "Poem for my son")
CIMARRON REVIEW, "The Sleep of Beasts"
COLORADO REVIEW, "One Step, Two Step"
CRAZY HORSE, "Elegy"
GREEN MOUNTAINS REVIEW, "Your Own Hour," "Father and Children"
HAYDEN'S FERRY REVIEW, "An Epiphany"
INDIANA REVIEW, "Rhapsody"
THE IOWA REVIEW, "Macular Degneration"
THE MISSOURI REVIEW, "Madrigal"
THE NATION, "Countdown"
NEW ENGLAND REVIEW AND BREAD LOAF QUARTERLY, "An Ecstasy"
NEW ORLEANS MAGAZINE, "A Letter to God"
NEW ORLEANS REVIEW, "Let Me Tell You About Happiness"
THE NEW REPUBLICS, "Round and Round"
POETRY, "The Boy Child," "Fathers and Sons," "Holy Family: Audubon Zoo,
          New Orleans," "Seascape with Attendant Premonitions," "The Soul"
PLOUGHSHARES, "Afterward"
PRAIRIE SCHOONER, "Child at Play," "Mother and Son," "Under Heaven"
THE SEWANEE REVIEW, "The Girl Before the Mirror"
SHENANDOAH, "Prime" (as "Matins"), "Texas Skyline"
THE SOUTHERN REVIEW, "Gravity," "To A Child Facing Out to Sea,"
          "Stepping In"
THREE RIVERS POETRY JOURNAL, "Soul Making," "All Souls' Day"
THE VIRGINIA QUARTERLY REVIEW, "Carousel"
WILLIAM AND MARY LITERARY REVIEW, "Wunderkind"
WILLOW SPRINGS, "The Choices," "A Dream of Childhood"

The author wishes to thank Alissa Cooley, Nicole Cooley and Jacqueline Cooley for their suggestions and criticism. To Rosemary Eddins and Sandra Haro of the English Department of Tulane University, particular thanks are due for their assistance.

Publication of this book is supported by grants from the National Endowment for the Arts in Washington, D.C., a Federal agency, and from the Pennsylvania Council on the Arts.

Library of Congress Catalog Card Number 91-72055
ISBN 0-88748-130-2
ISBN 0-88748-131-0 (pbk.)

Printed and bound in the United States of America
First Edition

CONTENTS

To my Mother and Father

"When I was a child, I spake as a child, I understood
as a child, I thought as a child: but when I became a man, I put
away childish things."

I Corinthians 13:11

A LETTER TO GOD

In the backyard the pear tree, Father,
has been my body. Today my daughters
chatter with dolls beneath it, cool,
washed by my shadow. If they knew. . . .

Years now the tree has gone on perishing.
Will you tell them? Someday will I?
How the air thickened with tiny wings
above my still, unripening cusps of scent
summer after summer; how the sky would streak
cobalt into ice while I would shake,
then call down harvests of black fruit.

What is a man that he keep himself
gnarled inside till his own terror
roots him in himself unspeaking?
These secrets my wife has never known.
But just this year we cried out the same moment:
that limb is gone, and it drew us together.

What other lives of hers could she but whisper
in the dead of night if I spoke first?
What beak or claw has she passed through,
what pinions fixed on azure?
What might we give words you had not heard before?

AUBADE

Coming down here to the river,
my daughter's fever broken in the night,
I walked inside the wind. I was cold, insistent,
shaking the burdock and the thistle,
the goldenrod and Queen Anne's lace
leveling and gathering their first shadows.
All the while, one crow called from the willows
coming into light while sumac reddened
toward autumn and the stones continued
maintaining the hill's direction as stones will,
spiraling down and down. Cold we began,
cold we went on. Below us, finally,
the river, emerald and purple, was nothing
but a string of barges or the floor of heaven
to either of us, wrapped in that morning's light.
As if deciding, the wind hesitated, racing in place
at the water's edge. And then, releasing me, it stepped out
to its own direction on the waves.
But just before that we had a second we knelt down.

THE CHOICES

Before they have conceived the son they hear him sing
strains they recall among the constellations.
By memory, therefore, they are led forward to the act.
All the long term at her blood the mother listens,
the father attends, skyward.
They teach themselves one flesh now, harmonious,
accompanied by expectation.
                                    The child's next song,
that pitch struck by his entrance, their babble
extinguishes. And next
they are too dissonant, at arms rehearsing names,
the choice they pour over his head,
for a note, even.
                    Still,
the gods release through him for a time
their clear unalterable musics
until the man and woman, allied, remembering,
set to work to tune the little one
on the wheel of language.

SATISFACTIONS

Sufficient a sky full of stars,
a sidewalk beside the hospital on which they fall
reflecting the weariness which leads him on.
Sufficient one step, then the other,
above which the body of the man
floats in obedience like a tide
divine and preordained. Sufficient
these celestials on their passage toward morning, yawning.
From their vantage point in time
the usual has happened again and they are tremulous
to hold each other, invisible, naked at last.
The man blinks, bleary and exalted.
Nothing comes clear but the store at the corner,
its last light sufficient to soon diminish
and the all-night gas station attended
by eyes two fists are keeping open
encased in a glass cage. It is three a.m.
Will the two men speak? Naturally not.
To the man walking home all the lights can threaten
blackout until the black holes blacken
all over again and a thousand candles
will wait for him, sufficient he is alone
breaking open the door to his own house
sufficient to no one, shouting
my son is born!

WUNDERKIND

From his crib at midnight
an infant sings to his dead sister,
the stillborn a mother and a father
gave second burial that day of his great birth.
He croons. This is why some newborns sleep
continually against their parents' rhythm:
they have their little ones to put to bed;
they have their memories of the long dread they have
        sailed from.
But the music which floods back, a cappella,
from that country at both beginnings of our lives,
breaks out sometimes in lamentation, rapturous.
I know. I have a wonder child.
And my sleeplessness pulls me down the undertow
where I wade depths only the lost forage
and resurrect, red eyes wild with oblivion.

A DREAM OF CHILDHOOD

Always there is a curtain
billowing with sun, a pelican adjacent
naming the air. From my crib
the voices down the hall swell to a water
which my small soul sails out,
father, mother, sister, a shoreline of applause.
I am accompanied, I am alone,
depending on the wind. Sometimes calm is all I ask.
Years pass. For all my races they are front row center.
I learn to come home, set trophies above the hearth. . . .
Here I can stop. Because it is all fiction, every line,
this dream is perfect, and may be called up
as now, whenever the wounds, especially pustulant,
squawk in their little nests. I clamp it shut,
down over their heads until the dreams' dead air
diminishes their lamentations. When it's done,
I lay them out, one by one, for a decent burial.

ALL SOULS' DAY

The moon calls, speechless, in her own language.
Here on the front steps I am her witness.
All evening in a white dress, hands extended,
she has been drawing the dead upward.
They flutter along the moonbeams, they stagger
after their long, hard day among us in the world.
And it is always like this: the children
as now, toward midnight, dawdling on their way to bed.
They are like snow when I reach to count them.
They frost my fingers, they vanish when I breathe on them.
This year, I think, the one of my own
has not come down with the migration.
There are ten minutes left until midnight.
There are ten billion little ones out here.
Yes, I guess this time oblivion kept her home.

IN ADVENT

Tonight I will suffer one star
to process above the others.
Suffer the flocks to cease
their bleating, lift one stare
skyward for the march.
Suffer the dung, the straw, the lowing,
the wise, the vessel of the mother,
the child, all one assembled at the crèche.
And then, no part of them, this young man
dumbfounded, kneeling in radiance.
Joseph, it is you I turn to
my twenty-three years a father.
You who have husbanded firmaments
yet come away convinced.
What trembling brought you to your knees
to take some other father's son
onto yourself, suspending everything?
At the edge of this page I bless your piety.
Suffer the myth to continue you
after I and my kind are gone.

HOLY FAMILY: AUDUBON ZOO, NEW ORLEANS

A mother, a father, a boy child, two years old maybe.
The lovers at the end of adolescence, when the glands
call to each other, demanding such oblivion
as only another can promise for a time.
Today, free day, they have left the shelter downtown
for a park bench before the lions, the boy standing above
      parents
so they repeat that trinity the quattrocento did to death,
though their poverty has probably something to do with
      oil
and there any connection to the Holy Land begins and
      ends.
I will see them later, younger, older,
beneath the expressway when I drive downtown to teach,
bartering something I've never tried with an old man
who lives there any weather. Or child and mother alone
may beg the steps where the legless woman squats
at the abandoned church until police chase them away.
And the father, face expressionless as the freshmen I face
      later,
can disappear in the Quarter and sell himself. So may his
      wife.
But one of them must keep the child, their savior,
alive and well so he will have a chance.
Listen to me! Preaching! Prophesying!
Probably the boy will be traded downriver or abandoned
in a shopping center I frequent after dinner
with my wife and son. We won't turn him in,
neither of us wanting any part of this. But someone will
and he'll appear, if he's charmed, in a special
at the end of the news which I turn off, exhausted,
bored or both, if grace descends to him.

MOTHER AND SON

I love this one more than my daughters,
she whispers to the goddess whose white beams
wash over the breast he suckles after midnight.
You, sister, understand. And the man
sleeping beside her, incidentally the father
of her conception, for two decades her husband,
sleeps the dead sleep, limbs strewn,
into which the male descends after his frenzy.
Tonight she gave herself to him for the first time
since the boy child came. Dreaming, she muses:
the infant at her breast could be the moon's
if she could sire sons from heavenly bodies—
she could float above the white face, the stars agog
as she rose and fell, woman over woman finally.

THE BOY CHILD

She is becoming that small hum
under her breath to which she will retire
the middle of a word, my aunt,
and stare out at her apple tree the autumn swells
wizening and brown with its last fruit.
At eighty-five she can hang there hours
on a few white notes while I come and go,
attending to the business of my visit
which is to check out that moment in her house
I've come back to all my life. I can report it's here,
the time she told me as a child
standing by the window that the falling light was mine,
I could take down the sky if I went out to it.
Of course, I have tried and failed, of course,
and what I have written she never reads.
Now I have brought her my latest child,
a boy even, and she's pleased with him
but as I said, retired.
From where she looks back all things
look alike, I guess, miraculous and level.

CANONICAL HOURS: FOR MY SON

PRIME

Across the crib bars, his damp curls
descending from the latitudes of sleep,
my son lifts toward me
the first light of morning in his face.
This is the minute and in it
I would tell him, if the radiance were less,
that like him I have flown
last night in another life
over wetlands, polar reefs,
over sanctums where the tusks and claws
have not been named.
That together we have known the hours
when our one soul sets out
under cover of a white wing,
back before we assumed these bodies
and our attendant miseries
and this bit of words in my mouth.
Instead I pick him up, squalling,
swing him up over the cage,
yelp-yelp-yelp-yelp
breaking clean from his throat.
Later, I will teach him like a man
to bite down on it, riddling everything.

SEXT

Beside your sleeping crib
a mourning dove buried from the noon
within our magnolia's ice white heat
pours out his grief. Or is it anger?
In spite of what your mother says,
I'll teach you, even if it's cold,
to follow fire before you weep.
A boy has that one choice. A man has all of two
he takes in imitation of such music:
tears, fists—sobbing or tearing down the sky.
Whatever you decide, when you leave me
let it be your way, but still take down my voice
far back, sequestered in an upper branch.
Tell yourself it isn't mine if you accompany it.

AN EPIPHANY

In rain, in January, my southern house is almost dusk
by three o'clock, washed in an old shellac
like a burnished masterpiece. Italian? Flemish?
The question to the oaks is windy, academic.
They wait like their forebears in a lush calm.
And the neighbor's bungalows, ghost-washed like mine
from steps to mansard, retain the fractured light
shining down everything: teal, amethyst, vermillion
stand at the window they would enter at a word
as if I were one of the old masters.

Then let me be one: here in my son's bedroom
speaking a circle of light around his crib
that I may be a worshipper in this psalm I frame to him,
marveling at the commonplace of his recent birth.
Let me paint his features where the window sends him
        beams,
a nimbus; let his sleep be surrounded
by a bray, a low, from animals invisible
until I give them breath; let me enter my own vision,
one of the Magi, extending myrrh and hommage.
Or as the rain shifts, an angel, chartreuse, violet
or a legion, all white, if it lifts. Or if it doesn't,
Joseph, the most benighted of all fathers.
Here I am, flooded with color, assuring myself
the rainbow at the window is a firmament of stars
pointing his way, assuring myself I will not die,
any lie, to keep myself astonished at this happiness.

FATHERS AND SONS

When the day comes my son looks through me
I will be ready as my father was not,
a father who took refuge that day in totem silence.
But now my son is too tiny even for the blind worship
I saw spark the eyes of a four-year-old
across the aisle last Sunday morning on the bus.
And the father, twenty maybe, skin blotched from the
      flask
he drew from his jeans each time we braked for a town,
swatted, as if he could bat away some ache,
every time the little one lay a hand across his chest.
Neither had stopped trading love when I got off.

I dream my son will arrive at epiphany, manly, violent.
It will strip him like a young brave
walking naked into the brush when his body
stops at its full height. It will last one night
and finish at dawn when he refuses to come home but
      must—
his own camp set up, the ground burned and staked,
the crossed sticks erected, the skins stretched to fit
that ancestral concept, a tepee of his own.
He'll be dressed unlike me in some hide he has tanned,
and about ready to parlay, whooping in place,
he'll call the powwow, meet me on the line,
attempt half the talking, midway between our camps,
dancing mad I'm his size, red-faced he wants me gone.
And then, on the verge of tears, he'll take one step back,
a signal my father's ghost stands between us on this
      earth.
This will be the moment I tell him he can wait—
he has time, no one is standing in judgment, no one
      will—
to take back the blow he would like to strike
if I spoke. I won't speak. I'll be my father standing firm,
refusing a son the blood of his own father.

AFTERWARD

Between his crib slats the baby fed on them,
a man, a woman, the white sheet they turned to,
the vows, the sweats they traded, gulping.
Afterward, someone in shadow got up,
put on the falling light, first footsteps of the rain,
returning only to help prepare their supper.
The other dozed before the window's streaming face
and woke and dozed, humming some little nothing.
This is the hour the child remembers all his life.
Not the afternoon they shattered—his rocking chair
overturned, then screams, the chandelier knocked
        swinging. . . .
but the time before eating he was alone and never hungry
in the quiet flooding toward him from a sleeping body.
Years later, remembering, it will never matter
whether it was mother or father at that hour.
I lie awake, satisfied to be nobody.
Never again will the rain come down so slow,
so quick in alternation. This is my last afternoon as one
        of them.
After that I was a boy, the stillness in me.

II

"Always inside me is the child who died,
always inside me is his will to die"
—Robert Lowell, "Night Sweat"

THE JOSHUA TREE

Squatting mornings beside his crib,
awash in first light while sleep tosses him,
I have sailed for centuries in my son's face:
back to the origin of the tree
outside our window, its dagger-shaped, its spine-tipped
        leaves,
named for his namesake when he arose,
a warrior against his enemies,
on some plain which had divided from a marsh
eons before in the primeval.
Back to the origin of the sun
which even as the day proceeds will slip
between the lineaments of clouds only to come again.
By such squints and hintings you reveal yourself,
Invisible, giving me this child as you gave yourself
just one and spoke through Him a little while.
Listen. In this hush I am whispering to mine.
Shh. Shh. Shh. Shh. Shh. I tell myself.
When he wakes up he will begin to leave you.

ELEGY

As if in imitation of its rhythm
a child dances by the sea at night.
How perilous this step she reaches for,
the tide low, the breakers threshing stars—
sky, spindrift, reflected on the dark water.
She cannot mimic it; she knows this.
Already my daughter's body is preparing
her second body, one to call her, stumbling, from herself.
Too soon now for her father she will question
all things but the moon's continual pull
through turn and undertow and counterturn,
all but the blood's continuous measure.

SEASCAPE WITH ATTENDANT PREMONITIONS

Beyond the last wave the gulls ascend
after they break the lapis lazuli of the sky
gathered in the gulf water. With or without catch
they swoop and enter the long glides they are noted for
on bas-reliefs in Florida shopping malls. They appear
    drawn
by threads not quite invisible and they rotate
so no one day perceiving them is quite the same.
I threw this figure out like the white crust
I pitched one bird this morning. I meant it
to catch up in all sincerity my parents' death
though they are eighty and in quite good health.
Today I will call them. I haven't lately.
After the short, strained conversation,
my skin will itch and prickle from the sun
I kept to myself. At forty-nine I haven't learned yet to be
    their child.

COUNTDOWN

Child again for a few minutes,
I follow my son tonight racing the shallows
where the great white heron comes to rest.
He has just begun to babble; he suspends it
for a race that monotonously fascinates—
first the bird, always ahead, dipping a monstrous beak
to feed or not feed every few seconds,
next the boy, his miniature legs torquing the wind
to close the distance the bird allows him now and then
only to open it again by taking wing.
Because I could watch this forever, I think
its whole duration lasts a poem's length
or less: three shadows one sometimes against the sand
        and sea
nothing interrupts, rebuilding each one its fine losses.

THE GIRL BEFORE THE MIRROR

Beyond her, at the park,
the swans are surrendering the last light, violet,
to the lagoon's black shallows.
Lovers, who kept the banks
trembling all afternoon, rise from the reeds,
divide the darkness as they scatter,
speechless giving up each other's touch.

But to the girl before the mirror,
framed in the instant, swaying gold
among the motes her face diminishes,
they are only what will happen later.
Here, at the last moment of her childhood,
she has come upon her beauty, dazzling,
and beside herself she cannot let it go.

Entranced, she takes her cheek in hand,
and someone's bones escape her fingers
like the sea floor she has dived for summers.
She lifts her profile against herself;
it is a frieze in marble; no, it is a veil,
it is a crown of light to which she bows
and then, head lowered, puts on, shuddering.

Outside this moment the boys lunge at
each other, bodies hardening, stumbling
back streets, alleyways. They barter words,
obscenities, every expletive Platonic concept
for their hunger, this rise they waited for
and bring down with a flask, a joint, or loneliness
they can know only with each other.

Soon the mirror will disappear, and night
will lie down where it hung, glittering.
The boys will separate to sleep. And wake,
bringing her words which enter her.
She will leave them. She will be left,
marry one but never tell him:
how when the light fell she arose,

her hair streaming, her skin wax
to any mask the years would bear her;
how her lines hardened there, collapsed;
how her mouth, slack, gave her up
to suffer herself, suffering itself.
And she was no one she did not know
her whole life as she assumed this.

GRAVITY

Most nights even the stars are snuffed
by the fretwork of gulf weather overhead.
Nevertheless, his bare feet spurs,
my son straddles my back and this sidewalk
is my track to gallop past neighbors' houses dark
at the end of the ten o'clock news. Gee up, gee up.
Together we are a centaur in some allegory of the
        heavens
and that planet, always turned from us, Diana,
is the unknown female who eternally can fascinate.
While at the window, our Alpha Centauri, his mother,
maintains vigilance, a star always in sight.
She doesn't have much patience with this mythic
celestial quest. Even now I hear her whisper,
It's past his bedtime, get that boy of mine inside.

And the pull of the earthlight is irresistible.

FATHER AND CHILDREN

Sometimes taking my son's hand at night
to lead him outside where the moon awaits us,
he dawdling, then toddling beside me, babbling,
the ghost child waits at the opening of the door.
She is dead, she is what only his mother and I
know about; she sits on the bottom step
spitting, *Get on it, I've been waiting,* shredding bark
from the azalea bush or tossing stones in her fist
at the streetlight, *You're late, that son of yours
held you up,* and she stands then, exposing a face
where I could weep as the clouds pass over it,
the eyes and mouth sockets of darkness moonlight sucks.
For Christ's sake, you haven't got forever,
she shouts, the shout echoing down the street
where all three of us start out, night after night,
to wear out my little one until I pick him up, nodding.
And she is always ahead of us and behind,
she is on all sides, spectral and tireless.
When we arrive at our door, she gives us the finger
with a fleshless hand dissolving in the streetlight's glare.
Tomorrow, if we're lucky, will be her night off,
she has time. She's got all oblivion to be jealous of him.

RHAPSODY

This light reflecting light within a child's face
approximates what they once called the holy.
Here at my son's nursery school, squatting a chair
beside him, a half-dozen lit like him
encircling our table, I am a celebrant.
Blue-smocked little priests, the boys and girls
hunch over their work to which my son invited me:
it is only the world they reshape out of their clay,
the cosmos as three characters they smash, remake
    again:
a man, a woman, and a snake this rolling pin
is handed me to imitate. All afternoon I do what I am
    told.
Meanwhile the radiance thickens toward rain
in the city outside, assuming I'll return
the same man. I will. But smaller, I hope,
each instant knocking on the next one to let me in.

CARROUSEL

Still in motion, at a still turning,
my son and I, lashing the white horse,
canter past his terror this afternoon.
Before that, our legs and arms had intertwined,
sweating the withers of a black one.
His heart beat time against my chest—
I lost breath, fell below the surface,
no one for a minute. And when I reemerged,
dripping, stunned, I counted
on the hurdy-gurdy melody to set me on the ground.
And then for its rhythm to help us choose
the white charger we whipped together,
something broken in the speech of each of us.
Later we could be just two mouths in the crowd
stuck on cotton candy. And later still, at home,
he sank into *Sesame Street*, telling his mother
he'd "been the best place." And here I am,
the white, the black one, racing in my words,
bloodying each other so I can get this down.

TO A CHILD FACING OUT TO SEA

This has no image in the visible,
the depths the whitecaps stir in you.
Later, between your father and your mother
you will toddle out and still later
take on the taunts of friends
bobbing and plunging under lightning.
And later still, after you dunk her,
a girl will surface, then another, between your legs.
But now, speechless, the high tide breaks
your memory of the ancestral shadow standing upright
shedding gills, the lungs swelling with wind
when the night descended and we split
our souls from the Great Soul of the water.
I suppose the waves must call to you,
Little One, come back, come back—
but how can I know, making all this up
in the world's language, your mortal father.

|||

"'Difficult ordinary happiness,' / no one nowadays
believes in you."
—Adrienne Rich, "In the Woods"

YOUR OWN HOUR

Before dawn our kitchen is awash in such soft gray
as the world outside relinquishes each minute,
branch by branch tipped by profusions of advancing
        gold.
I bend to the gas stove's sanctuary of orange light
to set my teakettle shivering upon it,
clutching the cold cup I will fill
with my second awakening to honey and orange pekoe.
In this house of our three children
soon to awake, greedy for the day,
I have risen to the habit of this hour
in which the stillness breaks and mends and breaks
only if I speak. Though I won't call them,
half a continent away my parents, too, are up
at 5:30 in their eighties, occupied,
keeping each other at a whisper. They began this, I
        imagine,
forty-nine years back at my birth. I'd love to call,
to ask can you sense less clearly or more
with your diminished hearing these mourning doves
I hear my prayers in every morning now?
And will the sun on your kitchen floor
be dazzling soon in instants, too? More dazzling still
as the hours of radiance count themselves down?

SOUL MAKING

A man takes his face into his hands,
hands which are a pool of water,
water from the faucet in the dawn-chill dark,
dark breaking up with the first birds,
birds warbling the cold pond in his palms,
palms holding him in clear reflection.
Reflection chills the man a minute:
minute, tremulous repetitions
repeating his words are falling from a tongue,
tongue bent like his knees, his hands uplifting,
uplifted. This is how a day begins,
beginning in the rhythms the water stirs,
stirring animal pools in my brain till I emerge.
This is how the I takes on the world.

STEPPING IN

Falling into sleep, my son this afternoon
departs from his three-year-old body
sprawled on the rug in his room.
Around him the February sun, shaken by elms
stripped in the indigo wind, enters, then leaves,
reenters his face, to shadow it, encase it.
Now he is waxen, the bones standing clean
as they will in rigor mortis when he's ninety
and laid out and I am less than this second
stepping in, covering him with his mother's worry.

Probably I'll watch the light pay its respects
from my entrancement, nodding on this side of him
till the blue panes cease the rhythms of their cleansing
and the wind dies down and wraps the house in night.
Probably one of us will shake the other, wake him,
and to be himself, probably, the other weep.

THE SOUL

In their ascent from the pavement
the ten white fingers of my soul
should be drumming out their thanksgiving
I'm still alive. But they're too scraped, shaking.
I stand up. Now my feet, too, prove it:
I'm here, the alley of the downtown Y.
On the rooftops of the tenements around me
it is the same night coming down
I've always known, though this time
the arm which reaches for my gym bag
could be a phantom limb, not mine,
while the full figure of myself against a wall
dances skeletal, dances, a wild man in the cave.
As if for the first time I am a man standing up. . . .
I notice the stars I count on have begun to pulse
since I lay down, belly-flat, crying
at his command while he stood over me
while he cried back, you Mother, Mother,
repeating it as he tore my wallet for ten bucks,
all I had, and left the credit cards
while the pistol in his fist shook like his voice
and then decided I will sit down to dinner
this evening at the table whose edges I can grip
that the wine, the bread, my wife and children
be seen above water when I rise to them,
my vision rinsed in a white light
I never asked for from a man, weeping,
putting his finger on nothing he could name
until he turned and ran and chose to spare me.

LITTLE ODE

On the other side of this poem a man is weeping.
A man letting it all out cannot do it like a woman
in the face of a friend, no matter what the reason,
or in a mirror or while vacuuming or dusting.
Later, he has no mascara to repair, no hair he can tease
    back,
no changed colors to urge smoothly about his hips.

Therefore, he will be grandiose and something of a fool
in the company of gods and weather,
stepping out to address his proper element,
shouting obscenities or, even worse, his poetry.
And the great good earth will sometimes listen,
the sparrows among dogturds and standing water
will lift their wings to watch him pass
and a small cheep go up along the curbstones
to acknowledge this brother brought so low,
the huge splotches curdling his softened grizzle,
the wind tasting absurd curses learned at ten.

I said: he cannot do it like a woman.
But look: sometimes the gods, weary of their immortal
    humping,
soften the blows he gives his face with April rain.
And listen: beneath his swagger, staggering,
they let him bawl to himself like a small boy at last
so he thinks himself restored, calls his babble a new man
while a muse takes up her pen that he get one new line
for a poem he drags off to his bed.
And the goddesses, unsatisfied now that their men are
    spent,
drain their cups of nectar in sweet hope of getting drunk
while the gods punch each other and shake their mighty
    fists,
witnessing this spectre of mortal happiness.

THE HISTORY OF POETRY

Once the world was waiting for a song
when along came this. Some said it was a joke,
funny ha-ha, but at the end too lachrymose
to last. Others that it was writ
holier than thou and should be catechized,
then set to turgid dirges, wept over
with gnashed fang, wrung palm.
The ancient declaimed it fad,
the young, old fogies' play.
Almost everyone agreed, except the children,
who didn't listen, it was kid stuff.

Centuries yawned and fell back, stuporous,
eons stretched out, soaking up beauty sleep.
Then one day a peasant, knowing he hurt too much,
remembered hurting too much, told his wife
he might have written it
if, in another life, he'd been born better,
at least literate.
And when the gods heard this
they hungered suddenly to become mortal
and join themselves with us in lecherous praise.
Thus hereafter follows the stories of their sins,
their cries made flesh by euphony and trope
they whispered to us that we take them down,
their great debauches, all made-up
that we should emulate with our blood, pay in blood,
while we, in the cheap seats, stomp the floor and clap—
all loss, all the fallible, all poetry.

"LET ME TELL YOU ABOUT HAPPINESS"

Quick, let me have it, I need the word.
But mine, not yours you soaked in honeysuckle,
then delivered to the front door this morning
where, unsuspecting, I answered in pajamas
to catch you unaware: shining, baby-blue gabardine suit,
blue tie, a little blue book in your hands,
the shiny gold letters promising secrets within
for those who admitted you. I didn't, of course.
But after I slammed the door I squinted
through the curtains to take in the '65 Ford,
its back seat a swarm of kids swaddled in blue
you would have let loose on my own and on my wife
had I given an inch. And her beside you,
a blue snood streaming with fuchsia ribbons,
shot me her index finger three times
(I thought of Him three times raising the Cross
before He ascended) and stuck her tongue out thrice.
And so began another Sunday in our funny kingdom.

ROUND AND ROUND

When I remember the flamingos, the pink, explosive
flaming of one and then another like blossoms in the
      tropics
as they process across their island at the zoo
and assume the water, never uttering a sound,
I am someone else. Then I'm a third man
to see the lagoon take that color and the wind, too,
stunned by their preening to the pulsing, heightened
      shade
the sun setting gives my skin the dead of winter.
And then I'm cut loose, watching these frail armadas
set sail for nowhere but the containment of human eyes
where they drift, no one, nowhere but in confines of my
      mind,
a life passing while being stared at by me alone.
This is one of the circles I run in. But I've got smaller.

AN ECSTASY

In Atlanta, a city I have only seen
within the terminal walls between my flights,
an extra hour tonight is given me again.
Now, rush hour, Friday, I choose the busiest concourse,
a chair that faces the stream. I cast my line
far out, baiting the hook with nothing
so I may end up with nothing while the evening
reduces to the jeweled lights of planes descending
ruby and emerald, planes ascending, then reduces
to a constellation on the ground guiding them in.
There's nobody here with my soul
I have to be accounted to. . . . Just hundreds, thousands,
passing me by while I reel out on my own,
the eternal at my hand when I surrender the whole line,

to take me where it will or won't, delirious.

ONE-STEP, TWO-STEP

Go it on one foot, go it on two,
the one acetylene, every toe and tendon,
what choices to spin a morning from,
little pigeon, you down to breakfast
in the dust, but first to bathe
below my window, your head like mine
lollygagging even at this task.
Such is the way a day begins,
lonely for company but hoping
no one will show up to pilfer
some few feet of the world
you've got to yourself, splashing around
in earth before the cats come,
before noon sun scalds the street
or later the kids rush home from school
to kick and spit and heave themselves at you
in the image of this self-same stuff
mothers have forbidden them to touch.
Dust to dust, your lice-ridden,
dappled and roseate wings beat a rhythm
confusing earth and heaven for the likes of me
who has no other way to get there—
wherever There is—but hobbling, both my wings
pulverized like I think yours are
and irreparable, irredeemable, or maybe both.

TEXAS SKYLINE

Let me speak to you of the soul.
But first let me tell you I am in Houston,
a hotel like a shopping mall
and our earth thirty stories below.
When I ascended I rose
not on the wings I keep folded
under my corduroy jacket—
no, I sped in a glass shaft beside men
chortling through toothpicks about fucking
and oil stocks, their vests and their Stetsons
fine-toothed cowhide and suede, men who jingled
games of pocket polo in a chorus,
singing of women who wanted it
and who didn't and they all did
it was agreed by my floor
as I squeezed out past a rich belch and a fart.

Tomorrow I will read my poems
to an audience of Western professors
attending to keep up their culture,
one generation away from their holsters.
For the trigger-happy, I will cut it short.
Meanwhile, there is my dark night
in Houston, bejeweled by skyscrapers
which never cease their glittering
along my window wall, there is my soul insisting he
        come out.
And now there is this cold delicious glass here
where these wings, resplendent in my reflection,
would turn to solid flesh the second I hit air.
It is the window my face writes and rewrites
among a thousand lights and promises
which are translated, translated back
smaller, multifaceted, gilt-edged.

I have only to open my hands
and the map on which my life is written
will tremble with sweat along the life line
as I extend them to draw my poems from that glass.
For this I have come to Houston,
that I keep my great audience with no one
but myself, here, at the last resort
America has dreamed from oil and natural gas.
The continent has constructed it that I sit down
in the next few minutes and begin
to transcribe the first words of this poem.

CARNAVAL DES ANIMAUX

Now the animals are incarnate in the memory
    my childhood turned to in Detroit,
        city spoked like a wheel

we were taught in school, city
    of chrome and glass which wrapped cars
        while the hands of men died in the wrapping

that the cars die to stockpile junkyards, city
    where earth reincarnates as metal melted
        down. This is what my favorite toys were
            composed of:

overpriced, postwar
    five-and-ten-cent store collectables,
        they made their glass case a Smithsonian

each week I pressed closer
    my tenth summer to buy another.
        The lion, the elephant, the camel, the giraffe:

how many lawns were cut, how many
    sidewalks swept after nagging,
        to be swept again after a sudden rain

that a quarter or two enter my pockets
    for an hour till I got downtown
        to set a beast free in my hand?

If I remember the lioness best
    it is not because she was first
        and distinctly female. This I claimed, too,

for the others and as the world was made
    by me, they were all my women, though I did not,
        as now, think about them so much

as dream their purchase and then their exile
     in the seraglio of my room. There were stories
          I made up for their ears of my exploits

in isles from *Treasure Island* or *Gulliver*.
     There were promises for their ears
          outrageous as the mating practices

I had read about for Tyrannosaurus Rex.
     Nights I clutched one in my palm in bed
          as the teenagers' car radios outside in summer heat

belted me a snatch of forbidden song
     across my loneliness to set it throbbing.
          I was happy, happy as a child can be for a while.

IV

"Terminate torment/Of love unsatisfied/The greater torment/ Of love satisfied"
                    —T. S. Eliot, "Ash Wednesday"

UNDER HEAVEN

I've been giving my terror to the blind sparrow,
the brother I met on a window ledge
we both came to at the late hour.

Jump, go ahead, he said, and when I didn't,
we each opened up, he showed me his wounds,
the one that runs, then the prize one, its luster like
        moonstone.

I tell him how cold the ground is
to us, the wingless, how a man
for love of women will cheat and lie,

betray his best friend, murder, play with sounds.
He nods, swears their music makes his soar.
And every day, he says, he has to take it

from the owl about rats he shrinks from,
from the oriole about his puny range,
from swans about the offal on his coat.

He warbles the high noons he kept
before the shrike tore out his sight,
when, luminous, he rose through them,

bodiless in light, light, light and light.
I insist the body is a cage—
our soul flies, crazed here, till we die—

later, another wind will come for us.
I press his beak to the chill on my shoulders
where the wings curled up in my last life:

I unfold their absence, the white pain.
Like this we go on so many nights,
surviving ourselves, in memory together,

perched here, bartering ecstasies,
song to wing, pinions to the cracked melodies,
under heaven, fathomless,

the night sky at the back of our breath.

SWEET ONES

The little rocking horse, its rider mustachioed,
sombreroed and vested in south-of-the-border shades
the earth will answer to in Mexico—burnt sienna, raw
        umber—
this is his favorite bibelot the Advent calendar
has yielded up: each day another plaything
seizable behind the doors he rips open:
a wooden angel, a shepherd, a luscious plaster wreath,
its cherries so ruddy he can't resist licking them.
The collector with his feather duster
goes over the edges of his storehouse for the children.
To his satisfaction, there are just twelve days left,
twelve shopping days until Christmas. . . .
so few days left to get the graves of the little ones
washed and scrubbed in the basement, to tidy up
the cute headstones he made from Popsicle sticks and
        twine
so he can visit them dressed as Old Saint Nick,
the Advent toys in his sack, his belly swelling
Christmas Eve. *My sweet ones*, he whispers,
I will not add more to my storehouse for your sake.
I will not pick up another girl at school as her uncle.
I want each one of you to get two trinkets on your grave,
        lovelies.
It would be greedy of me to desire more kiddies.
It would be wrong to ask for more earthly happiness.

THE SLEEP OF BEASTS

I am sitting alone among the silence of the animals.
The day is almost over, the zoo's feeding time is done.
And the couples, hand in hand, this mating ground
        attracts,
have gone home, along with the teenaged parents and
        their child
who is the aftermath, perhaps, of too much staring
        between bars.
Like the caged ones, the satisfied, I am waiting for the
        dark.
In the last of their fat shadows kangaroos sprawl;
the panthers are stalking, beyond hunger they stalk all
        night.
The flamingos among swans scud their narrowing
        reflections,
sated by expectations met, already half-asleep.
Now a concession stand slams windows down
on grills where grease is sitting still,
where grease will sit tomorrow
deadening another appetite. *Thirty minutes,*
I hear the grounds keepers' first call; soon they will holler,
fifteen minutes, ten minutes, five minutes. . . .
This evening for the first time the old yearning
is refusing, as it has never failed me,
to be satisfied by staring an animal square in the face.

Such peace as I have known has come to me in seconds,
haphazardly by resting on an angel's wing,
entering a woman, a bar of music,
a stanza, the tint which sings contralto
when indigo is set against scarlet in a frame.
I know that none of these, no one
is going to take me tonight. No spirit,
animal or human, will reach through me before first
        light,
pushing me down to the earth to process on all fours.
No one will take this tongue always repeating
every second thought, this mind with multiple
lusts beyond the body's. No one
will shut off this ticking anticipation behind my eyes.

When I leave, I am the last to go into the dark
and the grounds keepers keep cursing, following me out,
You're here too often, don't you know when we close?
What has failed me tonight, the animals, myself,
or the rite I counted on to prepare me like a prayer
for the savannas of sleep, the grasslands before dawn
where I could wander unencumbered by the soul?
The iron gate slamming behind me refuses answer.

CHILD AT A WINDOW

He won't be back till dawn, your old progenitor,
that thoroughbred on all fours you spur on
across the floor of the living room good nights.
And the other nights, average nights,
you're some lariat he swings the air with,
you're a sash, dizzy about his waist
while your mother grips the doorframe, sobbing.
Tonight again he dragged you back to douse
your head in shower spray with his,
the two of you naked, him mooing, whinnying
and you watch as his long white thing in its patch
of black hair stiffens, then shrinks when he is weeping.

You can squat here on your bed, your face
gathering the years to come when you repeat
this same morning ritual with your son
and only when you're old know a father comes back
always only when the day is breaking,
his son awake, his wife snoring for hours.
And only then know why a boy returns for more,
hugging the father's knees even after bruises open
to a kick from someone stumbling up the walk,
that stench to be craved later as rich thirst
stinking his cheeks, his shoulders, the sudden hands
which bear up a son to kiss him while he cries
after he hits and hits and hits and hits
while the little one stands, crying.

BROTHER FRANCIS EXHORTS HIS FORMER COLLEAGUE TO APPEAR AT HIS TRIAL

Dear Brother Luke: I write you from my cell.
I must confess it's not much fustier
than what we knew together at the Brotherhouse:
a mouse or two, damper, the floor chillier,
and, of course, no crucified Jesus bedecks the wall.
Remember your cozy visits to my celibate sheets
long after lights were out? We wore one of those
        blankets
nubby and even holey with our chafing
and more! I get hard just starting to recall.
I touch myself and I explode. And now the vision
        comes:
the scene I've told them I can't bring back
and won't unless you're with me in my hand. . . .
I lead the choirboys into the sacristy,
I tell them the Father desires it and all the saints
will rise with them in their glory the last day
if they will drop their pants. You know
how boys are: they follow like little lambs
the first boy to unzip. And I do nothing to them,
one after the other, you and I didn't do,
Brother, together, making the sign of the cross
each time I put one in my mouth.
Luke, I saw Christ descend in white and black,
a handsome chap, his shoulders pale and robed with
        sweat,
his chest hairs wriggling ebony over his pectorals.
He was a condor come down to bless my acts
and I knew I was elected to his kingdom.
Then one of the boys squealed to his mother,
another to his father, and the news spread.
Now they lock me here against the will of God.
Write to them, Brother, assure them
I have the blessing of the Bishop, even the Pope
or at least your cute little white nakedness
which will come forward as witness for me in the
        courtroom.

MOTHER AND CHILD

The mother's hand uplifted testifies:
all the witnesses to her own suffering have been called—
the blue contusion on the thumb, the broken life line
floating her palm, the nails bitten and split.
She stands before me at the grocery check-out
sow-eyed, sow-bellied, none too clean around the neck,
no more than nineteen, food stamps in her fist
before she releases them to hit the child.
And now I'm retrieving one book from the floor,
one from the counter, righting milk and day-old rolls.
And on the edge a boy, three maybe, swinging from the
    ledge,
who cries because he's hit because he cries.
He is a child. He loves his mother like himself.
It is against the laws of nature, the laws of state, to interfere.

CHILD AT PLAY

And when they start at dinner I go into the shack
at the back of my head. Neato! The door closes, round
like I remember from *Hansel & Gretel.* I'm okay when he
        whacks

his fist in her eyes, okay when the sound
echoes way back like some truck backfiring maybe
in the next block. And sometimes she'll pound

the silverware, bawling when they've got whiskey
in the big, green "Let's Party" glasses Grandpa gave us
last Christmas. And it makes Daddy sleepy

but Mommy cries instead and breaks more stuff
and once she went after him like the Farmer's Wife
while I watched from my shack. (I always hope she'll
        have enough

so she'll pass out after he's passed out.) Wow! The knife
jumped back and forth like in a cowboy fight
and in my shack I wasn't scared because my life

is what you call *damned* like the witch's and every night
I've got to keep saying my prayer to her,
calling her "Mother of God" and "Light from Light,"

the way Grandma taught me. And when I'm older
I'm going to let Mommy and Daddy in my house,
but first I'll allow them to munch on the gutters

of marshmallow and chocolate, nibble, nibble like a mouse
on the roof tiles of strawberry till they're good and sick
and ready to puke when I open my little house

once they're asleep and take my pick
of the best knives, the butcher one maybe and pick
till their brains are like stuff you upchuck and puke and pick.

MACULAR DEGENERATION

Something like radiance is crossing my wife's face.
She won't admit it. I won't press her.
Now, while they happen, here are the facts:
my son is staring up into his mother's eyes;
we are standing in the kitchen at the day's beginning,
half-asleep over mugs of chicory swirling with cream;
he has just barreled in, five today, demanding
a cup of juice from her, not me. Not you,
he repeats. Of course, she fetches it, obedient.
Of course, I awakened the same slavery in my mother,
the need to be commanded by a man-child who is other,
forty years back. What boy could ask his father
with a glance to be maidservant and Queen of Heaven?
Tonight I will type my mother a short letter
since she has written me the facts about her vision—
that there is no cure for progressive scarring
of the retina from five years back and now she reads
slowly with a magnifying glass. I will detail
the feats of her grandson at his birthday party,
leaving out this morning's epiphany. Of course,
the instant he was born she could foresee this moment
because in her eyes he is her son, diminished,
and it is no one's business now how she relinquished me.

ONE SUCH CHILD

"The night I died I heard a child crying
in the room below me. I was almost ready.
And the assembled, the nurses, my wife and son,
my grandchildren who had watched the doctor close my
       eyes,
stood back, stiffly now because some instruments
had drawn me back to my beginnings on their dials.

The cry: sea gulls in their swirling rise-and-fall
above seawaters after rainfall, starving,
will break the sky down, diving: it was like that.
The high notes called me as lightning to the sea floor
calls to tiny fish swimming in the blind dark.
A soul was coming to the world that I was leaving.
All I prayed for was one breath more
I never found to ask it: that last second which of us was
       I?"

MADRIGAL

It is always the same poem.
It should begin *O hear me Lord O*
and then music could dispense with all the words
and the euphony of speechlessness would praise for me.
But in practice that cannot come to pass.
There must be some theme like a catalpa tree this
      evening
lowering, adagio, the wind among its limbs
outside a kitchen window where the timpani of dinner
      plates resounds
as set down by a tired woman. There must be her
      husband splashing wine
into two glasses reflecting the oven's plucked brown
      wings
where juices hum their promise of largesse.
There must be words spoken by one or both which grate
      and clash
before the children who choose this moment to appear.
(Let there be one boy, one girl; no, two girls to fill it out.)
And the children must be outfitted in varied rhythms
swelling to crescendo as they enter
to compare with tremulous songbirds high up on the
      tree;
and the birds must be contrasted, gifted with proper
      names,
branches to highlight and counterpoint their luscious
      tones.
And then an image must be drawn out of the tree itself
while I count on the wind to bring everything around,
the night falling so a listener will know I made this up,
and take not too lightly how it resolves,
missing thereby the still essential harmony and
      dissonance
which was His answer when I began to speak.